Contents

About the Author v

Preface vii

Glossary xi

1 Preliminary Strategies 1

2 Individually Oriented Management Systems 7

3 Group Oriented Management Systems 25

4 Using the Techniques—A Final Word 34

References 41

What Research and Experience Say to the Teacher of Exceptional Children

Series Editor: June B. Jordan

Series Editorial Committee: Carolyn M. Callahan, Herbert T. Goldstein, Alice H. Hayden, Merle B. Karnes, Thomas C. Lovitt, Joseph S. Renzulli

Other published titles in the Series:

- Early Childhood
  Merle B. Karnes and Richard C. Lee
- Developing Creativity in the Gifted and Talented
  Carolyn M. Callahan

Titles in the Series in preparation:

- Reasoning Abilities of Mildly Retarded Children
  Herbert Goldstein and I. Leon Smith
- Discrimination Learning
  Alice H. Hayden
- Affective Education
  William C. Morse
- Assessment and Individual Programing
  Edward L. Meyen
- Social Acceptance and Peer Relationship
  Maynard C. Reynolds
- Instructional Technology
  Wayne D. Lance

About the Author

Thomas C. Lovitt, Ed. D., is Professor of Special Education, Experimental Education Unit, University of Washington in Seattle. Currently teaching graduate classes in special education, he has worked with mildly handicapped students in the Missouri public schools. The focus of Dr. Lovitt's many publications, including books, articles and monographs, has been on learning disabilities and on interpreting research for teachers. Among his special professional interests are basic skills teaching, the use of applied behavior analysis methodology with learning disabled students, and inservice education with regular teachers and teachers of mildly handicapped children and youth. At present, Dr. Lovitt is the Principal Investigator at a Child Service Demonstration Center, a Title VI Learning Disabilities Program involving both public school classrooms and university settings.

Preface

As long as there have been schools there have been mischievous children. But do not be alarmed, it is not my intent to trace the history of disobedience in the schools. Neither is it my purpose to survey the methods used by teachers to deal with those behaviors.

According to the testimony of teachers, school children have a handsomely varied repertoire of disruptive acts. They have spoken without asking permission and roamed about their classrooms without the approval of their teachers. They have sassed their teachers, tattled on their mates, and threatened their enemies. They have thrown rocks, torn papers, climbed walls, and kicked the floor. They have cried, whined, lied, cheated, and stolen.

A teacher's reasons for being irritated by these performances are equally varied. A few admit that they are annoyed by the noise and confusion. By the end of the day no amount of Excedrin can calm their frayed nerves. They yearn for environments that are quiet and restful. Others are irritated by these violations of law and order because they believe the offenders are harming themselves. They maintain that the obstreperous youths would be better able to read, write, or compute if they talked out of turn less and stayed in their seats more often. Many are annoyed by recalcitrant children because they claim that the educational opportunities of others in the class are infringed on by the noise and confusion.

Some teachers are more troubled by these inappropriate behaviors than others. A few fly into a rage at the slightest infraction. Others are more lenient; they can tolerate more noise and confusion. Not only is there a wide range of tolerance from one teacher to another, but each teacher has an individual range. On some days they can cope with a great number of irregular behaviors; but on other days the least disturbance strikes painfully on sensitive nerves.

Throughout the years, school teachers have reacted in various ways to these inappropriate behaviors. Some have scolded, others have threatened or punished misbehaving children. A few resorted to shaming and sarcastic approaches. Others have pleaded and lamented when children misbehaved. Many have sought outside assistance by calling in principals, parents, psychologists, or psychiatrists. Many have simply given up; they either quit teaching or resignedly counted the days until their current class would graduate.

For whatever reason or reasons, some teachers are more successful than others when it comes to managing inappropriate behaviors. This is apparent to the most casual visitor to a school, who can observe that in one room the children are quiet, hard at work, and often raise their hands when they wish to move about or speak. But in the room next door pandemonium may reign. The children are running about, talking, and laughing; there is no discernible order or system.

There can be little doubt that the struggles between some teachers and their children will long continue. To my knowledge, nothing has happened recently that would ease the pressures between these perennial antagonists. In fact, during these times when more people are concerned about disciplinary practices in the schools, more law suits are directed toward teachers for various reasons, more youngsters are encouraged to express freely their views and objections, and more citizens are aware of school practices in general than ever before. It would also appear that maintaining order is bound to become an increasingly difficult task for all concerned.

Coupled with these factors, which are certain to put pressures on teachers to deal quickly, firmly, fairly, yet humanely with inappropriate behaviors, the plight of regular teachers will be compounded by the mainstreaming process. Since one of the basic provisions of Public Law 94-142 is that children must be educated in the least restrictive environment, scores of handicapped children must now be returned to regular settings.

Heretofore, many of these children were enrolled in classes for the learning disabled, mentally retarded, or emotionally disturbed. Many had been evicted from their regular classes because they had behaved inappropriately. And, although certain of their behaviors may have been decelerated when they were in these smaller, special classes and their teachers used systematic contingencies, many of those behaviors are likely to reappear when they are sent to larger classes where the rules are more liberal.

The intent of this monograph, then, is to help teachers to manage disruptive behaviors. An effort will be made here to provide a number of strategies that may be useful in establishing peaceful situations.

In the first section several approaches are discussed that pertain to the general, comprehensive management of classes. There appear to be certain pedagogical features that teachers should incorporate whether or not they have disruptive children in their classrooms. Likewise, some strategies for increasing the motivational levels of classes are described in the first section.

Included in the second section are several strategies that may be used with individuals who display inappropriate behaviors. Here the reader will find techniques for managing entire classes or small groups of children whose behaviors are disruptive. The final section contains concluding remarks about the management of disruptive behaviors.

Research from the applied behavior analysis literature has been used to support the recommended management strategies. *Applied behavior analysis* is used as a generic term that subsumes operant conditioning, behavior modification, precision teaching, and responsive teaching. The primary methodological features shared by these systems are direct and continuous measurement. *Direct* implies that the behavior of concern is precisely defined and subsequently counted. *Continuous* refers to the fact that the defined behavior is counted over a period of several days. A number of explanations of this system have been published. A particularly good article is by Baer, Wolf, and Risley (1968).

Glossary

Attenuate. To weaken or decrease the frequency of a behavior.

Baseline. That period of time during which the conditions are natural, nothing has been altered. This phase is used as a benchmark from which subsequent interventions are evaluated.

Consequence. That which is given or taken away as a result of a contingency arrangement. A consequence refers to an item or event.

Contingency. Refers to the temporal arrangement between a response and a consequence. That is, if a certain type of response occurred, then something would happen.

Decelerate. The same as attenuate; to weaken or decrease the frequency of a behavior.

Extinction. A procedure whereby the frequency of a behavior is lessened by first identifying the reinforcer that maintained the behavior, then withdrawing the reinforcer.

Overcorrection. Exists if the frequency of a behavior is decreased when a person was required to correct the inappropriate behavior and perform that behavior within a natural sequence of events.

Principle. A basic law or truth. In this book, principles have been distinguished from events or techniques. The latter are those specific tactics used to alter behavior, whereas a principle is a collection of events or techniques all of which have similar effects on behavior. For example, the principle of positive reinforcement means that when an event or technique was granted contingent on a behavior, the rate that behavior occurred was increased. Several events might be reinforcing: praise, free time, books, or model airplanes.

Target behavior. The behavior of concern; the topic behavior of a project.

1 Preliminary Strategies

There are at least two preliminary strategies that should be employed by teachers in their efforts to establish harmonious classrooms before they schedule individual or group oriented **contingencies** to decelerate behaviors. They should do everything possible to arrange attractive and motivating classrooms.

ATTRACTIVE CLASSROOMS

There are several features of the average classroom to which teachers should carefully attend. It is my belief, and this is supported to some extent by research, that when these aspects are properly dealt with, many irksome behaviors will not emerge. This is not to say, of course, that if the features presented here are implemented, all inappropriate behaviors will vanish. It is to suggest, rather, that when the classroom atmosphere is intelligently managed, many disruptive behaviors will be prevented. Such a strategy might be compared to the preventive measures of other disciplines that have reduced the intensities of many situations and forestalled the emergence of many others. Following are five features that should be implemented in order to prevent a rash of inappropriate behaviors.

Attending to Esthetics

My first recommendation is that teachers should make classrooms as appealing as possible. Let's face it, some classrooms are very bland, boring, irrelevant, and humorless. In some situations the same bulletin boards have been on the walls for 10 years; there are no plants, pets, or posters. In other rooms the same daily schedule is followed throughout the year, the only deviations being for fire drills. The instruction in some classes is related neither to this life nor to the hereafter. Some teachers never smile, much less crack jokes. They have taken literally the message that education is a serious business. This search for the attractive is extremely important when we consider that children and teachers must function in these rooms for 5 or 6 hours a day for 9 months of the year.

Stating Goals

Teachers should clarify their positions in regard to acceptable and unacceptable behaviors. It is important that they and the children know precisely what is expected. Sometimes teachers themselves are not certain which behaviors they want children to exhibit and which they will not tolerate. Understandably, many children in those situations are woefully confused.

If teachers do not want their children to roam about the room or talk without asking permission, they should explicitly state those expectations. They must specify precisely all those behaviors they do not want to occur in the classroom.

Accordingly, teachers should tell the pupils which behaviors they do want them to exhibit. If they are to begin their assignments promptly, work on them continually throughout a period, complete them before the allotted time, and finally, request more work, teachers should clearly outline that sequence of activities.

After teachers have listed precisely all the "do's" and "don'ts" they should reflect on the wisdom of these choices. They must analyze every item and determine whether they are simply trying to channel their youngsters into ancient and perhaps non-negotiable molds, or if they are truly "doing what is best" for them.

If, after teachers have evaluated the items, they have decided on certain revisions, these revisions should then be explained and discussed with the class.

Changing Teacher Behavior

After teachers have presented these lists to their children, they should behave accordingly. That is, alter their own behaviors. Obviously, teachers should praise, or in some other natural way reinforce, their pupils for exhibiting the behaviors they should and ignore, or in other ways extinguish, those behaviors they should not exhibit.

Most teachers do not automatically behave in this way. All too often, if pupils do something on the approved list they do or say nothing, believing, apparently, that the students obviously should act in this way, and since they should, they receive no commendation. On the other hand, when pupils do something on the "no" list, teachers are likely to attend to the behavior by reprimanding, threatening, or insulting.

Establishing Rules

The fourth approach teachers should use is to establish a few rules—only a *few*, however. Furthermore, they should attach some consequences to those rules. They should be contrived in respect to the most important or troublesome aspects of the classroom.

If a teacher believed that the most important behavior in the class was for the children to complete all their assignments, a rule with a contingency in reference to this desired end should be drafted. The teacher might specify that if the pupils did not finish their work by 3:30, they must take the unfinished tasks home and complete them there. The teacher might state also that the pupil will not be allowed to come to school the next day unless the homework is completed. (If such a contingency were established the teacher must be certain that school is a fairly reinforcing place.)

Although teachers have always laid down certain rules for their children, they have not always been successful in achieving compliance. There are, I believe, at least two reasons that might account for some failures. First, some teachers make too many rules; there are so many rules that the children quickly become confused and exhausted in their attempts to comply with them. They begin to ignore certain of the decrees, then others, until finally, they ignore the classroom code totally. Another reason some rules do not successfully alter behaviors is that **consequences** are not prescribed. A rule without a consequence is as feeble as the sound of one hand clapping.

When there are too many rules, children quickly become confused and exhausted in their attempts to comply with them.

Involving the Pupils

Whenever possible the pupils' viewpoints should be considered when classrooms are being organized. In common practice, teachers make all the decisions. They determine the seating arrangements, the behaviors that are to be taught, and how and when the pupils will be instructed. They ordinarily specify all the rules and the contingencies.

If one of the objectives of the educational system is to train people to become independent and be able to survive and perpetuate our democratic form of government, they should be allowed to have a part in determining many aspects of their academic lives. Some research has strongly suggested that children are highly motivated when allowed to manage certain components of their academic routine (e.g., Lovitt, 1973).

MOTIVATING CLASSROOMS

The belief is shared by many and supported by some research (e.g., Ayllon & Roberts, 1974) that a number of inappropriate behaviors can be curtailed if pupils are engaged in academic exercises. To conjecture that all disruptive behaviors would be alleviated by a strong emphasis on the development of school related skills would, of course, be sheer fantasy. Nevertheless, it is highly probable that many disruptive behaviors would be prevented and others greatly tempered if students were motivated to the extent they worked on various academic tasks.

Following are several options teachers might consider in their attempts to arrange motivating situations. (The material in this section is adapted from Lovitt, 1977.) As a word of caution, teachers should be careful when they arrange reinforcers, particularly those that are expensive or habit forming. Ordinarily, once a reinforcer is used to change a behavior, it should be removed as soon as the behavior has changed. Like a medicine or any other therapy, a reinforcer can, if used unwisely, effect a cure that is worse than the problem. With these warnings in mind, a ranking of different types of reinforcers is now presented. They are ordered on the basis of expense and naturalness.

Arranging Two Simultaneous Behaviors

One approach of this type would be to arrange one academic activity contingent on another. A situation may be devised whereby the pupils earn the privilege of engaging in one academic activity if they perform up to standard in another. For example, if a student naturally enjoys reading but his arithmetic is poor, he may be allowed to read from a favored book if his arithmetic performance is accurate or surpasses a prescribed rate.

Another technique for building two behaviors simulteously would be to arrange some pupil management activity contingent on academic performance. For example, if a pupil's reading or arithmetic performance reached a certain level, then he would be permitted to see or make the daily plot on his graph. Several other pupil management components might be contingently arranged, such as scheduling, counting, specifying objectives, and specifying contingencies. In instances such as these the pupil would acquire proficiency in some basic skill and at the same time learn about graphing techniques, measurement, and the development of independence.

Contingent teaching is another technique that can be used to develop two behaviors simultaneously. Many children love to play school. Just as often, teachers need help because they cannot give their assistance to all their pupils. One way to arrange such a situation would be to permit a pupil who was having trouble with a skill to teach a younger child that same skill. If, for example, a fourth grader who was having trouble with his reading wanted to teach a first grader, it could be arranged that if the older child's performance was acceptable, he could then work with the younger child for a few minutes a day.

If none of these techniques proved successful, that is, if situations could not be arranged whereby the student developed two behaviors at the same time, still other approaches must be considered.

Arranging Socially Acceptable Behaviors

One technique of this type would be to give increased recognition to the child of concern. Several examples of this approach may be cited. One would be to allow the student, contingent on her performance, to talk with a favored person. Another would be to allow the child to display a graph of her performance, a picture she drew, or her arithmetic sheet in a favored place contingent on performance. Still another approach would be to give the pupil notes or send notes home contingent again on her performance.

A second technique of this type would be to allow students to do certain things in the classroom, contingent on performance. They might earn such privileges as erasing the chalkboard, being first in line for recess, choosing a song during music class, selecting the game during recess, being a team captain, or distributing papers.

A third recourse would be to grant leisure time contingent on performance. There are at least two ways in which this can be done. One is to allow pupils to do almost anything they want at their desks when they have completed a prescribed task. If the pupils finish their arithmetic assignment satisfactorily, they can remain at their desks and draw, read, or color. An alternate approach is to arrange, in the classroom, a leisure time area, in which there may be games, toys, and records that are appealing to various children. Pupils can gain access to this area only by performing some academic behavior at a specified level of acceptance.

5

Considering Token Economies

The third type of motivational situation is the token economy. There are many variations on this theme, but the basic elements are that pupils are first given a mark or an actual token contingent on performance; later, those awards are redeemable for books, games, toys, or whatever. Some of these systems do, in fact, help students learn, but they are invariably costly. Furthermore, the research to date is discouraging in regard to subsequent maintenance of performance once these systems are removed.

Arranging Tangible Rewards

The fourth motivational approach, and the most expensive to operate and difficult to remove, is the direct granting of some tangible reward item, contingent on performance. In the early days of behavior modification the favored "reinforcer" was the M & M. These candies were fed to children contingent on all types of behaviors, from walking to reading. Many other rewards such as cookies, soda pop, and model airplanes have also been contingently arranged in efforts to modify behaviors.

A final note may be added by way of summary. In the selection of reinforcers, the manager should begin with the first type and move up, avoiding the most expensive and most difficult to obtain if possible. If it is ultimately determined, however, that a pupil will not develop a desired behavior unless an expensive arrangement is used, that arrangement should, by all means, be scheduled.

2 Individually Oriented Management Systems

In this section, various approaches for dealing with individual problem behaviors are described. First, some techniques are explained whereby something is given in order to **decelerate** the target behavior. Following this, various techniques are described which require that an event be taken away.

GIVING SOMETHING TO ATTENUATE A BEHAVIOR

Five approaches used to **attenuate** a behavior are described in this part. They have in common the feature that something was given when either the target or another behavior occurred, in an effort to decelerate the frequency of the **target behavior.**

Giving Aversive Event Contingent on Target Behavior

When this method is used the manager presents something to the pupils when they engage in the target behavior. Several applied behavior analysts have arranged this procedure, among them were O'Leary, Kaufman, Kass, and Drabman (1970). The subjects in their study were two boys, members of a regular second grade class. Throughout the project the boys were observed for 20 minutes a day during an arithmetic period. Observations were made every 30 seconds of several disruptive behaviors: out of chair, touching other's property, vocalization, noise, aggression, and time off task. Each day the mean frequency of disruptive behavior was graphed. That frequency was calculated by dividing the total number of disruptive behaviors by the number of intervals observed. Throughout the investigation the number of teacher reprimands was also counted.

In the **baseline** phase the teacher exercised her normal procedures to manage the children. Since few soft (individual) reprimands were given during that period, it was referred to as the loud reprimand condition. The data from that period indicated that the mean frequency of disruptive behaviors was quite high for the two boys.

During the second phase the teacher used soft reprimands. When a child was disruptive, she spoke only to him; no others heard her. The frequency of disruptive behaviors greatly decelerated for both boys.

Throughout a third phase the teacher gave loud reprimands, and during a fourth condition she gave soft reprimands once again. The data from those periods were similar to those of the first two phases; the frequencies went up when the reprimands were loud, and down when the reprimands were soft.

In this study, O'Leary et al. discovered that the frequency of reprimands was not constant throughout the four phases. The teacher censured the pupils fewer times in the soft than in the loud phases. Therefore, a second study was arranged, during which the frequency of reprimands in all conditions was controlled. The data from that investigation were similar to those of the first.

◆

When this method is used, the manager presents something to the pupils when they engage in the target behavior. . . . In those instances when this technique was effective . . . it would attain principle status and be referred to as *punishment*.

◆

A second project of this type was conducted by Hall, Axelrod, Foundopoulos, Shellman, Campbell, and Cranston (1971). The pupil in their report was a 7 year old girl in a classroom for profoundly retarded children. The behavior of concern was pinching herself or someone else. The frequency of those behaviors was recorded daily.

During a 6 day baseline phase no specific technique was used to reduce the number of pinches. Throughout that phase she averaged 71.8 pinches per day. In the next condition the teacher pointed a finger at the girl and said "no" in a loud voice each time she pinched. The average number of pinches in that 18 day period dropped to 5.4 a day.

A brief third phase was scheduled during which time the baseline procedures were reinstated: the teacher did not point or say "no." The rate of pinches rose to an average of 30 per day. In a final phase, when the contingency was again instituted, the girl's average rate fell to 3.1 per day.

Other researchers have decelerated behaviors by giving some event contingent on the target behavior. Risley (1968) used this procedure to control the excessive climbing of a brain injured girl, and Corte, Wolf, and Locke (1971) used it to eliminate self injurious behaviors.

In those instances when this technique was effective, that is, when the target behavior was eliminated or decelerated, it would attain **principle** status and be referred to as *punishment*. A functional definition of this term would be a technique that decelerated the frequency of a behavior when it was given contingent on that behavior.

It is illustrated in the studies described here that soft reprimands and saying "no" were punishing to children. Other children might be punished by frowns, reminders, and other subtle expressions. Those events, when contingently arranged, can decelerate a wide range of behaviors, from talking out of turn to being late for class.

The primary advantage of punishment is that when used appropriately it can immediately reduce or eliminate a behavior. One disadvantage is that the effects might overgeneralize: more behaviors might be eliminated than the teacher intended. Furthermore, there is danger that the student might associate the technique with the person who administered it and consequently, withdraw from that individual.

Giving Something if Frequency of Target Behavior Is Low

When this technique is used the teacher gives some consequence to the pupil if the frequency of the undesirable behavior is lower than a specified level.

A study which used this approach was published by Dietz and Repp (1973). The pupil in their project was an 11 year old boy. He was classified as trainable mentally retarded and was enrolled in a special education class. According to his teacher he was the most disruptive student in the class.

The topic behavior throughout the study was talk outs. Those incidents included talking without permission, singing, or making statements not related to the ongoing class discussion. Data were recorded for 50 minutes each day.

Throughout the 10 day baseline no specific techniques were attempted to decelerate talk outs. On the average, 5.7 occurrences per 50 minute session were recorded.

In the second phase the definition of talk outs was explained to the pupil. He was told, also, that if he talked out less than four times during a session, he would be given 5 minutes of free time near the end of the day. During that phase he talked out about once each session and, therefore, always earned the free time. The contingency was withdrawn in a brief final phase. Subsequently, the pupil's rate of talk outs increased slightly.

Dietz and Repp conducted two other experiments during which the same contingency was arranged with groups of children. There were 10 trainable youngsters in one study. The behavior of concern was again talk outs. The students in the other project were 15 senior high girls. The topic behavior was off task verbalizations. In both studies the technique of giving free time if the frequency of the target behavior was low proved to be effective.

Hall, Fox, Willard, Goldsmith, Emerson, Owen, Davis, and Porcia (1971) also used this method with a 13 year old girl in a junior high classroom for emotionally disturbed children. Her teacher reported that she displayed a number of inappropriate behaviors, including walking around the room, talking out of turn, hitting others, and throwing objects. Since her talk outs were particularly bothersome, that behavior was defined and each occurrence was counted during a 30 minute period each day.

During the first phase the teacher did not attend to her talk outs in any particular way. There were, on the average, about 67 infractions a day during that 10 day condition. In the second phase the girl was shown her graph. In addition, the teacher praised her if the number of talk outs was fewer than on the preceding day or if the frequency of the behavior remained at a low level. She averaged about 8 talk outs a day in this 9 day phase.

---◆---

When this technique is used the teacher gives some consequence to the pupil if the frequency of the undesirable behavior is lower than a specified level. . . . When it is effective . . . it is called *differential reinforcement of a low rate of responding* **(DRL).**

---◆---

In the third condition the girl was not praised for low frequencies, but praise was reinstated during a brief fourth condition. These data showed that her talk outs increased in the third phase, but were nearly eliminated in the final condition.

This procedure has been used in other studies to reduce behaviors. When it is effective, and thus achieves principle status, it is called *differential reinforcement of a low rate of responding* (DRL). Although several scientists have used this approach in basic laboratory investigations, few applied studies have been reported.

Teachers might consider using this technique in situations where they hope to reduce the frequency of a behavior to a tolerable level. DRL could also be used to eliminate, by stages, disruptive behaviors.

This technique might be used to diminish most of the troublesome behaviors. Out of seat occurrences, for example, might be dealt with. An arrangement between the teacher and pupil could be agreed on whereby the pupil was awarded free time or a favored activity if he was out of his chair fewer than a specified number of times. DRL could be used to reduce the number of times a student went to the bathroom, the drinking fountain, or the pencil sharpener.

A disadvantage of DRL might be that in those instances when the target behavior was gradually suppressed, it was not eliminated quickly enough. Some behaviors might be extinguished more quickly if teachers simply tried to eliminate them suddenly and completely. Time and energy might be lost if teachers lowered their expectations too gradually.

Giving Event Contingent on Nontarget Behavior

When this technique is used, the teacher should first identify the target behavior, then give a reward periodically when that behavior does not occur. Sometimes the teacher can identify and give something for a behavior that is the opposite of the target behavior. At other times the teacher would specify a range of behaviors, all of which were more appropriate than the target behavior. She would then give the pupil a reward if one of those behaviors occurred.

―――――◆―――――

When this technique is used, the teacher should first identify the target behavior, then give a reward periodically when that behavior does not occur. . . . (When) the technique is effective . . . (it) is appropriately labeled as *differential reinforcement of other behaviors* (DRO).

―――――◆―――――

A study that used the former approach—giving a reward for an opposite behavior—was reported some years ago by Sloane, Johnston, and Bijou (1967). The subject in their investigation was a 4½ year old boy whose behavior featured an abnormal amount of extreme aggressiveness and excessive fantasy play. The study took place in a remedial school for children with behavior disorders.

Throughout the project, fantasy play and appropriate play were recorded. Fantasy play was defined as explicit verbal statements in which the boy referred to himself or others as imaginary characters, or actions that carried out these roles after they were expressed. Appropriate play was defined as those periods when the boy talked about himself and did not construct an imaginary scenario for his playmates. A 10 second, time sample recording technique was used to obtain the data. Each day two plots were graphed: percentage of fantasy play and percentage of appropriate play.

During the 19 day baseline period adults generally entered into the boy's fantasies. They willingly played the roles designed for them. On the average he engaged in fantasy play 35% of the time, whereas he played appropriately only about 39% of the time.

The interaction procedures between the boy and adults were altered throughout the second phase. At that time the boy received no social reinforcement or attention if he entered into fantasy situations. Instead, he received attention when he played normally. Toward the end of this period he engaged in appropriate play about 60% of the time; he was involved in fantasy situations only about 2% of the time.

Throughout a final phase, social reinforcement was given intermittently to the topic child and the other children in the group. The percentage of time he engaged in appropriate play steadily increased throughout that condition; on one day his score reached a peak of 80%. His time spent in fantasy play continued to be brief; on the average about 3% of each session.

Hall, Lund, and Jackson (1968) conducted a study that illustrated the alternative method for arranging this technique. They specified a range of behaviors that were different from the target behavior and reinforced those if the target behavior did not occur.

The student in their investigation was a first grade boy who displayed several disruptive behaviors. He made loud noises, got out of his seat, and talked with other students.

Some common sense should be considered when the reinforcement of nontarget behavior approach is used.

Throughout the project a counselor obtained data relevant to his studying and being disruptive. Every 10 seconds the boy's behaviors were evaluated. If he was studying or being disruptive during an interval a mark was made. At the end of each session these calculations were transformed into percentages and graphed.

During the baseline phase, the teacher neither reprimanded the boy when he was disruptive nor reinforced him for studying. The data during that 7 day phase indicated he was generally disruptive.

Throughout the second condition, the teacher praised him occasionally when he was studying; she did nothing when he was disruptive. These data showed he was disruptive about 2% of each session during the 12 day phase.

The teacher no longer praised him for studying in the third phase, but responded favorably to his studying in the final condition. These data indicated that his disruptive behaviors increased to 3% in the third phase, but dropped to less than 1% in the last period.

Throughout the project the percentages of time spent studying were inversely related to the times the boy was disruptive. In those phases in which he was praised for studying, he attended to his academic tasks more often than during the conditions in which he was not praised. Some comments are provided later about the relationship between academic performance and other, nonproductive behaviors.

Other researchers have used this technique to decelerate behaviors. Peterson and Peterson (1968) arranged the procedure to eliminate self destructive behaviors; Becker, Madsen, Arnold, and Thomas (1967) to reduce classroom behavior problems; Repp and Deitz (1974) to extinguish agressive and self injurious behaviors.

In those instances during which the technique is effective—the target behavior is eliminated or reduced—the technique becomes a principle and is appropriately labeled as *differential reinforcement of other behaviors* (DRO). DRO is defined as a technique that decelerates a behavior when behaviors other than the target behavior are systematically reinforced.

Teachers might use this approach with a wide range of behaviors. If, for example, a teacher desired to reduce the talk outs, out of seats, or swears of a child, he might first identify a reinforcer, then give it to the child when she raised her hand before speaking, stayed in her seat, and spoke appropriately instead of engaging in one of the target behaviors.

An advantage of the DRO approach is that the individual may be reinforced for engaging in a wide range of behaviors, with the one specified exception. It is also an agreeable approach. Most supervisors would support teachers who planned to use DRO; whereas they would not approve of other procedures.

A possible disadvantage of the DRO might occur if the teacher did not specify carefully the range of behaviors other than the target behavior that would be reinforced. In those instances it is possible that a behavior worse than the target behavior was reinforced, whereupon a situation worse than the original was created.

Giving Event and Related Events Contingent on Target Behavior

When this procedure is followed the pupil must correct his inappropriate behavior. Furthermore, he must execute the behavior within a sequence of other behaviors.

Phillips (1968) used this technique to decelerate the number of times a boy said *ain't*. The youngster was a member of Phillips' Achievement Place, a home for boys who had committed minor offenses and had histories of academic failure.

Throughout that study the number of times the boy said *ain't* was recorded for 3 hours each day. During the 10 day baseline phase neither contingencies nor instructions were provided for his grammar. On the average, he said about 7 *ain'ts* per session.

In the second phase a correction procedure was initiated. During that period a house parent interrupted the boy's conversation if he said *ain't*, informed him of the error, suggested an alternative, and

───────────◆───────────

When this procedure is followed, the pupil must correct his inappropriate behavior ... (and) execute the behavior within a sequence of other behaviors. ... (If) the technique is effective ... (it) is labeled *overcorrection*.

───────────◆───────────

required the boy to repeat the sentence using the correct word. During this phase he said as many *ain'ts* as he did in the baseline. His average, throughout this 20 day period, continued to be 7 per day.

In the third phase, which ran for 29 days, the correction procedure was continued. In addition, a 20 point fine was levied each time he said *ain't*. Throughout the study, points were redeemable for bike riding, television viewing, and other activities. The data from that condition indicated that the combined procedures were effective. On the average, he said only 3 *ain'ts* per day; none were said the final 15 days of the phase. Data obtained 30 days after the completion of the study revealed the inappropriate word had not reappeared.

Foxx and Azrin (1973) also reported the use of a correction technique to eliminate certain behaviors. In that investigation their clients were four severely retarded or autistic youngsters who were 7 or 8 years old.

The study was conducted in a playroom during the children's entire 6 hour day at a day care center. The experimenters focused on one of four behaviors for each child: object mouthing, hand mouthing, head weaving, and hand clapping.

The sequence of procedures for the first three behaviors was as follows: baseline, correction, baseline, correction and verbal warning. For the fourth behavior, a baseline, correction, verbal warning sequence was scheduled.

During the baselines, no particular instruction, feedback, reinforcement, or correction technique was in effect. Throughout the correction phases the procedures depended on the target behavior. For mouthing objects, the child was told "no," and required to brush his teeth and wipe his lips with a washcloth each time he put a potentially harmful or unhygienic object in his mouth. For head weaving, the teacher restrained the child's head, then instructed her to move her head either up or down, or look straight ahead. If she did not move her head, the teacher helped her to do so. She was then required to hold her head stationary for 15 seconds. This training continued for 5 minutes. The procedure for hand clapping was similar to the head weaving sequence. Contingent on each clap the child was instructed to move his hands in one of five positions. If he did not comply, the teacher manually guided him. When his hands were in position he was required to hold them there for 15 seconds. After that period another instruction was given. The training continued for 5 minutes.

During the verbal warning condition the children, after the first occurrence of a behavior, were told not to commit the behavior. Thereafter, if the behavior occurred, the correction procedures were implemented.

The data from those reports indicated the correction procedure was effective with all four children. For example, the percentage of time that one girl mouthed objects was significantly influenced by the technique. During the baseline phase she mouthed objects on an average of 80% of the time. When the correction technique was used the percentage decelerated to 5%. In the third phase, when the procedure was withdrawn, the percentage of time she put objects in her mouth went up. When the correction technique was reinstated, however, the percentage again dropped. The percentage of time continued to be low when the verbal warning was used.

Other investigations have been published that support the use of this procedure. Azrin and Powers (1975) used the technique to reduce the disruptive behaviors of a group of emotionally disturbed boys, and Epstein, Doke, Sajwaj, Sorrell, and Rimmer (1974) to decelerate inappropriate hand and foot movements.

In those instances when the technique is effective, it is elevated to the role of principle and is labeled **overcorrection.** A definition of this procedure would be that it exists if the frequency of a behavior decreased when a person was required to correct the inappropriate behavior and perform that behavior within a natural sequence of events.

One of the advantages of overcorrection is that it may be used with a wide range of behaviors. Another advantage is that the technique is rather benign; few supervisors or parents would criticize teachers who used it. A possible disadvantage could be that some behaviors might be modified more quickly if other, more direct, techniques were scheduled.

Giving More of Target Event

If teachers use this technique they should actually give the subject more of the event they ultimately wish to eliminate.

Some years ago Allyon (1963) published a report that illustrated how this technique could be arranged. The subject in his study was a woman who had been in a psychiatric institution for several years. The behavior of concern was the hoarding of towels. Although many efforts had been made to discourage her excessive accumulation of towels, she continued to collect them. Periodically, a nurse went to her room and brought several back to the store room.

Throughout the study, data were kept in respect to the average number of towels in her room each week. In order to ascertain the amount, a nurse went into her room when the woman was not there

◆

If teachers use this technique they should actually give the subject more of the event they ultimately wish to eliminate. . . . When this approach is successful, it may be referred to as *satiation.*

◆

and counted them. During a baseline period, when no special procedures were in effect, there were generally 20 towels in her room each week.

During the second phase of the study the nurses began taking towels to the patient's room when she was there. They handed stacks of them to her and left. Throughout the first week they delivered about 7 towels each day; by the third week she was given 60 towels a day. When the number of towels in her room reached 625 she began returning a few. In the next few days she carried more and more towels back to the storeroom until there were only two or three left in her room each week. Thereafter, she was satisfied with only a couple of towels in her room at a time. This was considered a normal number.

When this approach is successful, it may be referred to as *satiation*. The reason for presenting data for an older person in a psychiatric ward rather than offering an example of a young child in a school situation—the approach followed for the other sections—is that I could not locate any research of the latter type. This is not too surprising, because a teacher or other manager would need to be highly skilled in order to arrange this technique effectively.

Nevertheless, satiation could possibly be scheduled to decelerate several behaviors and indeed, some teachers have a fair understanding of its efficacy. Children caught chewing gum may be required to chew dozens of sticks until they are tired of the process. This procedure may also be used to reduce talk outs. Children who talk out of turn may be required to stand in front of the room and orate for several minutes. The technique could also be applied to out of seat behavior by requiring youngsters to remain out of their chairs for long periods of time.

Obviously, a great advantage of this technique is that the tactic to be associated with the inappropriate behavior is readily apparent. Teachers simply give more of the behavior they wish to eliminate. A corresponding disadvantage would be that the frequency of the target behavior might actually increase. If the pupil were given more of the target behavior, e.g., opportunities to remain out of seat, he might be highly reinforced, and the teacher would now have to deal with a far more serious problem.

TAKING AWAY SOMETHING TO ATTENUATE A BEHAVIOR

Three techniques are described in this section. In each instance the teacher took something away from the pupil in an effort to decelerate a troublesome behavior.

Taking Away Opportunity To Obtain Reinforcement

When this technique is arranged the teacher must deprive the pupil of a reinforcing environment. A study that illustrates this technique was published by Clark, Rowbury, Baer, and Baer (1973). The subject in their research was an 8 year old girl who had been diagnosed as a mongoloid. The study took place in a preschool classroom for problem children.

Acctrding to her teacher the child displayed several disruptive and dangerous behaviors. Three of those behaviors were recorded throughout the study: chokes and armwraps, attacks toward people, and attacks toward materials. Those behaviors were recorded every 10 seconds throughout a 60 minute period each day. A given category of behavior could be scored only once per 10 second interval. The data were graphed in order to show the number of 10 second intervals per hour that contained the disruptive behaviors.

A multiple baseline design was chosen for the study. During the baseline phase the teacher ignored all disruptive behaviors and attended to the girl when she engaged in nondisruptive behaviors. Occasionally, however, she attended to the girl when it was necessary to stop her from hurting another child. During that period chokes and armwraps were recorded, on the average, during 15 intervals. Generally, there were 15 intervals during which attacks on other people were noted, and 6 intervals during which attacks on materials occurred.

In the second condition the contingency was associated with only chokes and armwraps. Whenever the subject engaged in a behavior from this category she was placed in a booth and the door was closed. She was released after 3 minutes, provided she did not cry or bang on the door during the final 15 seconds of the period. During that time the frequency of chokes and armwraps was greatly reduced. Meanwhile, the frequency of the other behaviors increased.

Throughout a final condition the same procedure was in effect for all three behaviors. The number of intervals per hour any of the behaviors occurred during that period was very low.

During a second experiment Clark et al. investigated the effects of intermittent schedules on the procedure. The same pupil was used in this experiment and the same behaviors were recorded. The results indicated that some intermittent schedules were as effective as the continuous schedule that placed her in the booth after every inappropriate behavior.

Some years ago we conducted a project employing the same technique (Lovitt, Lovitt, Eaton, & Kirkwood, 1973). The principal youngster in the investigation was a 9 year old boy. The setting was a class for learning disabled children.

Throughout the study the teacher recorded the frequency of inappropriate verbalizations. These generally pertained to sexual or bathroom topics. During a baseline phase that ran for several days, no special technique was programed. Following each remark, the teacher generally frowned and told the pupil that he should not use such language in the classroom. On the average, there were about three outbursts each day. On one day there were seven.

During the baseline phase the teacher observed that the subject enjoyed chatting with a young man who sat next to him. Apparently they were rather close friends. This relationship was the key to the subsequent intervention.

Prior to the treatment phase the teacher talked with the subject's friend and asked if he would help with an experiment. He agreed. The teacher then explained that from now on whenever the subject uttered an obscenity he should tell the subject he did not like sitting by him when he used that type of language. The friend was also told that after he had informed the subject of his displeasure, he should pick up his books and move to a chair some distance from the subject. In addition, he was instructed to return to his chair near the subject after 20 or 30 minutes. After his return he could chat quietly with the subject if he talked about appropriate topics. The data throughout this condition indicated the removal technique was effective. After a period of two weeks there was rarely an instance when the subject uttered one of his choice remarks.

This approach has received considerable attention in applied behavior analysis journals. Using this technique, Watson (1972) attenuated the cries and whines of a student, Briskin and Gardner (1968) reduced several inappropriate behaviors of a young child, and White, Nielsen, and Johnson (1972) suppressed several of a youngster's deviant behaviors.

When this technique is effective and becomes a principle, it would of course, be referred to as *time out*. Time out has been defined as the removal of a source of reinforcement contingent on a response, and once that reinforcement was removed, the frequency of the target behavior was diminished.

In order to use time out the teacher must first identify a reinforcer. She must then deny the individual's access to that reinforcer, contingent on the target behavior. If, for example, the teacher discovered that being in the classroom was reinforcing to a child, she might send the child from the room, contingent on a behavior she wished to depress. Similarly, if a teacher intended to decelerate the frequency of a behavior and determined that a particular event, location, or person was reinforcing, she could remove the pupil from one of those situations contingent on the target behavior.

An advantage of this approach is that once a reinforcer has been identified and arranged appropriately the probability is great that

---◆---

When this technique is arranged the teacher must deprive the pupil of a reinforcing environment. . . . When (it) is effective . . . it would . . . be referred to as *time out*.

---◆---

the behavior will be decreased. A possible disadvantage of time out is that a pupil might be inclined to pair the aversive consequence with the administrator.

Taking Away a Portion of Some Event Contingent on Target Behavior

When this technique is used the teacher should withdraw some reinforcing event from the pupil contingent on an undesirable behavior. Hall and associates (Hall et al., 1971) published a study that exemplifies this technique.

In that investigation the pupil was a resident in a home for emotionally disturbed boys. Throughout the study three behaviors were recorded: cries, whines, and complaints. They were recorded during a 30 minute reading and a 30 minute math period. During the baseline condition no special technique was scheduled in either period. On the average, six target behaviors were recorded during reading and seven during math.

Throughout the next phase a contingency was scheduled only during the reading period. At the beginning of each reading session the boy was given five slips of paper with his name printed on each. He was told that one slip would be taken from him each time he cried, whined, or complained. In that period the frequency of the target behaviors was generally zero during the reading periods. Meanwhile, the rate of those behaviors increased during the math periods.

In the next phase the slips were also taken away during the math period. These data indicated that the frequencies of the target behaviors were low in both classes. Following this phase a condition was scheduled during which the baseline procedures were again in effect. In that period the frequencies of the identified behaviors increased in both classes. Throughout the final phase the withdrawal contingency was reinstituted. The target behaviors rarely occurred in that phase.

Iwata and Bailey (1974) conducted a study with six elementary age special education students that featured a take away contingency. One of the purposes of this study was to compare the effects of giving or taking away tokens on inappropriate behaviors and an

---◆---

When this technique is used, the teacher should withdraw some reinforcing event from the pupil contingent on an undesirable behavior. . . . When this technique is effective it may be called *response cost*.

---◆---

academic task. A second purpose was to determine which procedure—giving or taking—was preferred by the youngsters. A third purpose was to study the effects of using either procedure on the rate at which the teacher gave positive and negative comments to the students.

The study took place during a 40 minute mathematics period. Each day several measures were obtained. Off task behaviors and rule violations were recorded every 10 seconds. Likewise, the approving and disapproving comments of the teacher were recorded every 10 seconds. At the end of each period the number of math problems completed and the percentage correct were recorded.

During the baseline phase a tape cassette, programed to deliver a signal on the average of every 10 minutes was brought to the class. The children were instructed to begin their math assignments when they heard the first signal and continue for 40 minutes.

Throughout the second phase paper cups were placed in front of the six students. Three of the pupils were given 10 tokens in their cups. They were told that if during any interval between signals they were off task or violated a rule, one token would be taken away. No tokens were placed in the cups of the other three students, who were informed they would be given a token for each interval they were on task and obeyed all the rules. All of the students were told they could earn a snack at the end of the math period if they had at least six tokens.

Throughout a third phase the cups, tokens, and snacks were no longer in effect. After a few days, the token program was reinstituted. During that latter phase the contingencies were alternated for the youngsters. Those who were given tokens initially had to earn them and those who earned them were now given tokens. In a final phase the children could select each day whether they would be given the tokens initially or would have to earn them.

The data indicated that both techniques—giving or taking away tokens—were effective. Moreover, they were equally effective. During these conditions when the tokens were used the children were on task a greater percentage of the time and violated fewer rules than when tokens were not available. Furthermore, they completed more math problems with greater accuracy during the token conditions than during conditions when they were not given.

As to preference, the selections were about equal. Surprisingly, the pupils chose the take away contingency as often as the earning arrangement.

The data indicated that teachers dispensed the same number of disapproving remarks in either give or take away circumstances. Teachers were more inclined to praise, however, when they gave tokens.

A few other investigators have arranged this take away procedure to decelerate inappropriate behaviors. Kaufman and O'Leary (1972) established the technique to reduce disruptive behaviors and Phillips (1968) to attenuate aggressive statements and tardiness. When this technique is effective it may be called *response cost*.

Classroom teachers might use response cost to eliminate behaviors other than those mentioned here. The technique could be used to decrease talking, swearing, teasing, or hitting. It might be used to reduce name calling, tattling, tearing papers, or any number of behaviors.

An advantage of response cost is that many objects may be taken away: slips of paper, tokens, points, minutes of recess. Furthermore, they may be taken away immediately after the behavior occurred, as in the Hall et al. study, or after a period of time, the procedure used in the Iwata and Bailey investigation.

In some studies tokens were given freely, then taken away contingent on inappropriate behaviors. In others, children earned tokens which later were taken away. In some instances negative side effects were reported when tokens were taken away that had been earned.

One disadvantage of using response cost was noted earlier. It may be that when this procedure is used, teachers do not give as many approving remarks as they might if other procedures are used.

Taking Away Attention Contingent on Target Behavior

When this technique is used the teacher should ignore all occurrences of the target behavior. This approach was used by Williams (1959) to attenuate a behavior. His study was perhaps the first behavior modification study conducted by parents.

The subject in his report was a 21 month old boy who had been seriously ill for much of his brief life. Although he was in good health at the time of the study, he continued to demand the special care and attention he had received over the many critical months of his life.

The little boy was particularly demanding of attention at bedtime. Ordinarily, if one of his parents put him to bed, then left, he screamed and fussed until a parent returned. As a result, someone generally stayed in his bedroom until he went to sleep. This vigil was maintained from 30 to 120 minutes each night.

After the parents were reassured by a doctor that their child was in good physical condition and did not need their constant presence at night, they decided on a different tack. They elected to place the boy

―――――◆―――――

When this technique is used the teacher should ignore all occurrences of the target behavior. . . . When this technique is (effective). . . it may be labeled *extinction*.

―――――◆―――――

in bed, kiss him good night, leave the room, and close the door. If he cried they would not return. On the first night that this procedure was followed the boy yelled and screamed for 45 minutes before he finally went to sleep. The parents adhered to this approach on succeeding nights, and by the seventh night the child did not cry at all when placed in his bed.

A few weeks after the nighttime routine became more pleasant, an aunt came to visit. One evening while she attended the boy, he fussed after being put to bed. The aunt rushed immediately to his aid and remained in the bedroom until he went to sleep. Regrettably, it was necessary to reinstitute the ignoring technique. Once again, the parents placed the child in bed and left the room. The first night he cried and screamed for 52 minutes. By persevering for seven days, however, the parents eliminated his crying for a second time.

Another study that used this technique was conducted by the Zimmermans (1962). Their study, like Williams', is a classic in the literature of behavior modification. The investigation, which took place in a residential treatment center, was perhaps the first published behavior modification study in a special education setting.

The subject of their project was an 11 year old boy. The behavior of concern was spelling. The boy's teacher reported that when he was called on to spell a word he made faces, stalled, and pronounced a series of unrelated letters. While he engaged in these nonproductive behaviors his teacher ordinarily coaxed him to spell the word, asked him to sound out the word elements, and gave him a series of cues. Finally, after considerable time had been spent, he would generally spell a word correctly. The teacher noted that over a period of 10 or 15 class sessions, when this solicitous approach was followed, the boy took increasingly more time to spell each word.

After several weeks the teacher altered her procedures. During the new phase she asked the pupil to come to the chalkboard and spell some words. She then pronounced the first word and waited patiently until he spelled it correctly. He whined, fidgeted, and misspelled the word about 10 times. The teacher was firm, however; she ignored all his inappropriate behaviors. When finally he wrote the word correctly she immediately looked at him, smiled, and said "good." She then pronounced the next word. Once again he squirmed, moaned, and broke his chalk a few times before he wrote the word correctly. The teacher pronounced 10 words to the boy that first day. He required successively less time to spell each one.

On the following day, the teacher continued to use her new technique. She gave attention in the form of smiles and conversation contingent on correct spelling but ignored any behavior that did not contribute to good spelling.

Several behaviors have been altered by this technique. For example, Wolf, Risley, and Mees (1964) reduced the throwing of glasses; Carlson, Arnold, Becker, and Madsen (1968) curtailed tantruming; and Hart, Allen, Buell, Harris, and Wolf (1964) eliminated crying. When this technique is appropriately used—the frequency of a behavior is lessened—it may be labeled **extinction.**

Several classroom behaviors might be dealt with effectively if the teacher first identified the reinforcer that maintained the undesired behavior, then pulled away the support. If, for example, some of the children tattled, argued, or complained and the teacher normally reacted to those behaviors by pleading, cajoling, or threatening, he or she might, instead, ignore those behaviors. In other instances, particularly with older children, youngsters are more reinforced by their peers than by adults. In those situations a teacher might deal indirectly with certain disruptive behaviors by reinforcing some of the children for ignoring the inappropriate behaviors of others.

One advantage of using extinction is that it can be an extremely effective technique, particularly when a desired incompatible behavior is simultaneously reinforced. Another advantage is that the effects are long lasting, generally more so than when other decelerating techniques are arranged.

Two disadvantages, however, are often associated with this technique. One is that the frequency of the behavior at the onset of extinction is occasionally higher than prior to its use. The teacher must be prepared for this initial worsening of the behavior. A second disadvantage is that, ordinarily, the target behavior is reduced only gradually. If a sudden effect is desired, other techniques would be more appropriate.

3 Group Oriented Management Systems

Occasionally teachers have been assigned classrooms that are in a state of absolute chaos. They may have implemented the preliminary strategies recommended here, and the class remained intolerable. When they attempted to identify the troublemakers there were several; it was impossible to isolate only two or three offenders. Since there were so many misbehaving children, a teacher might speculate that were he or she to concentrate on one youngster at a time, it would require several months before the classroom would be manageable. In instances such as this, teachers might consider group oriented management systems. Following are three approaches that have been successfully used.

INDIVIDUAL CONSEQUENCES, CONTINGENT ON INDIVIDUALS

When this technique is used the same behavior for each member of the group is identified. Each child receives the same consequence when he or she engages in the behavior. An example of this technique is the "timer game," a tactic designed by Wolf, Hanley, King, Lachowicz, and Giles (1970).

The youngsters in their study were 16 low achieving children in a remedial classroom. Of them, 14 were fourth graders and 2 were from the third grade.

Throughout the study the out of seat behaviors of the pupils were recorded. These behaviors were recorded every 30 seconds for 1 hour each day. During each interval the observer surveyed the class and noted which children were out of their chairs. Each day the average number of out of seat occurrences per hour was plotted.

During the baseline phase, the timer game was not in effect. In that 7 day period the frequency of out of seat events was extremely high.

Throughout the second condition, which lasted 6 days, the timer game was used. During that period a kitchen timer was set to ring on the average of once every 20 minutes. Each student who was in his seat when the timer rang was awarded five points which could be redeemed later for snacks, clothes, or field trips. During this phase the average number of intervals the children were out of their seats was reduced significantly.

Following this phase, baseline procedures were reinstated; the game was no longer in effect. Throughout this 7 day period the number of out of seat responses increased to the level it had been during the first condition.

McAllister, Stachowiak, Baer, and Conderman (1969) also used this management system. The pupils in their investigation were high school youngsters in two English classes. There were 25 in the experimental group and 25 in the control group. Throughout the study two behaviors—talking out and being out of seat—were measured in both classes.

These data were gathered for 60 minutes each day. An observer in each class made a determination every minute whether or not a talk

---◆---

When this technique is used the same behavior for each member of the group is identified. Each child receives the same consequence when he or she engages in the behavior. . . . Arrangements such as these . . . (have been referred to) . . . as *independent group contingencies*.

---◆---

out or out of seat incident had occurred. If any student committed one of those behaviors during an interval it was noted; further occurrences of the behavior in that interval were not recorded. Daily percentages of intervals for talk out and out of seat events were graphed for both groups of children.

During the baseline condition the teacher functioned in her usual manner as she conducted both classes. That condition lasted 27 days for the experimental class. Following that period the teacher focused on the inappropriate talk outs in the experimental class. Whenever an incident occurred she responded with a direct, verbal reproof; she generally referred to the offender by name. The same consequence, therefore, was in effect for all students.

After the reprimand procedure had been in operation for 26 days for talk outs, the same technique was used for out of seat occurrences. During that period, the same direct, verbal consequence was used for both inappropriate behaviors. Throughout the study the individual consequences were scheduled for only the experimental, never the control, students.

The data from this study indicated that the individual reprimands were successful. When the technique was used first for talk outs, these decelerated. A similar lessening of the behavior was apparent when the technique was arranged for out of seat incidents. Meanwhile, as the behaviors of the experimental pupils were altered, the behaviors of the control youngsters remained at about the same levels throughout the study.

Litow and Pumroy (1975) referred to arrangements such as these as *independent group contingencies*—each member's consequence is dependent on his performance. Several other studies have been conducted in which the same consequence was arranged for the same behavior of all group members. Birnbrauer, Bijou, Wolf, and Kidder (1965) used a token economy, Schutte and Hopkins (1970) used teacher attention, and Osborne (1969) used free time to modify several classroom behaviors.

Teachers have commonly established independent group contingencies—the same rules for all children. The following have been practiced for years; "anyone who chews gum must stay after school"; "anyone who talks out of turn too often will miss recess."

An advantage of this contingency is that many would declare it was a fair procedure: the same rule for everyone. It is also an easy contingency to administer. When the target behavior occurs, the teacher knows exactly how to react, regardless of who committed the behavior.

Some might argue, however, that this is an unfair contingency in that it does not consider the individual competencies of pupils. Some children, for example, are initially more hyperactive than others. If the same rules are enforced for them as for the quieter students, the argument goes, the former may become discouraged, frustrated, and even more hyperactive.

GROUP CONSEQUENCE, CONTINGENT ON INDIVIDUALS

This system is established if the same consequence is given to all members of a group. In order to receive the consequence, a selected member must perform at or better than a specified level. Wolf et al. (1970) used this contingency with an elementary age girl in a remedial classroom. Throughout the study they recorded incidents of being out of her chair.

During a 90 minute period an observer tallied whether or not the behavior occurred. Each day, the percentage of intervals during which out of seat behavior took place was graphed. In the first condition, which lasted 20 days, no systematic procedures were followed. She was out of seat much of the time during that period.

In the second condition the timer game was used. It was set to go off on the average every 10 minutes. Prior to each session in this phase the child was given 50 points and told she would lose 10 each time she was out of her seat when the timer sounded. Her performance was greatly influenced in that phase. During that time she was rarely out of her chair.

A peer contingency was arranged throughout the third phase. During that period the girl could earn points both for herself and for the four students who sat closest to her. The arrangement was identical to that of the preceding phase. Each day she was given 50 points at the beginning of the period and 10 of them were taken from her each time she was out of seat. During this phase she was required to share the points that remained at the end of the session with her four mates. If, for example, she had 40 points after a session, she and each of her chums received 8 points. Her out of seat activity was nearly eliminated in that condition. There were no occurrences on 7 of the 9 days.

In a fourth phase the individual point arrangement was reinstituted. In this 9 day period the number of out of seat incidents increased slightly.

During a final 17 day phase the group point arrangement was reinstated. The number of out of seat occurrences was reduced to the level of the first group phase.

―――――――◆―――――――

This system is established if the same consequence is given to all members of a group. In order to receive the consequence, a selected member must perform at or better than a specified level. . . . This procedure has been referred to . . . as a *dependent group contingency*.

―――――――◆―――――――

Brooks and Snow (1972) used a modification of this system with a 10 year old boy. He allegedly displayed several inappropriate behaviors, among them stealing, leaving the classroom without permission, and not staying with his classmates during physical education, music, recess, or lunch. According to his teacher he stole during those periods. The teacher reported that it was difficult to control his stealing because he was rarely caught, and reprimands had no effect on his pilfering. Furthermore, his stealing was reinforced by some of his peers who traded him items for certain purloined goods.

Baseline data were obtained to reveal the number of times he left the group without asking permission. The data indicated that he wandered away from his mates on the average of 7.5 times a day. During that phase it was estimated that he stole something once or twice each day.

Following that 5 day baseline the teacher explained to the class that the boy had difficulty finishing his work and staying with the group, and, furthermore, he took objects that belonged to others. She asked the class, therefore, to help him and informed them he would be given a point when he did one of the following:

1. Completed his academic assignments.
2. Remained in the classroom for a 45 minute period.
3. Stayed with the group during an activity outside the classroom.

She also told the class that when he accumulated 10 points the entire class would be given 15 minutes of free time, but they would lose a point each time he behaved inappropriately. In addition to these group consequences, the target pupil was given 10 cents for every 10 points he earned.

The data during this condition indicated the procedures positively influenced the boy's behaviors. He earned a reward for his chums each day, and, as a result, they gave him a great deal of reinforcement for his benevolence. Furthermore, he neither left his classroom nor another area without permission during those days and, as a result, there were no reports of stolen goods. It was also noted that he completed all his assigned tasks—quite a change from his production before the group oriented system. In addition, the teacher reported that the quality of his work had improved immensely.

In the "group consequence, contingent on individuals" technique, a selected member must perform at or better than a specified level.

After a week the program was discontinued. Data on all the dependent measures were taken 6 weeks later, however, and periodically throughout the remainder of the school year. Those reports indicated, happily, that the deviant behaviors had not recurred and the boy's academic performances continued to be satisfactory.

This procedure has been referred to by Litow and Pumroy as a *dependent group contingency*. Other researchers have used this contingency to decelerate behaviors. For example, Kubany, Weiss, and Sloggett (1971) used the system to reduce disruptive behaviors of a first grade boy and Greenberg and O'Donnell (1972) used it to eliminate the tantrums of a 6 year old boy.

Teachers can arrange such group oriented contingencies to reduce several inappropriate behaviors. Not only might the behaviors dealt with here be eliminated, but the system might be employed to extinguish talk outs, hits, tattling, and a wide range of irksome behaviors.

An advantage of this contingency might be that certain behaviors of the peer group would change for the better at the same time that a behavior of the target youngster was modified. For example, the peer group may have initially reinforced inappropriate behaviors of a youngster. Later, when a group oriented system was established, it became more profitable for them to support his appropriate behaviors. In those instances when the peer behaviors were altered by the contingencies, they gained as much as the target child. Such was the case in the Brooks and Snow investigation.

Another advantage of this contingency might be that when some individuals are placed in positions in which they can provide events for others, they are reinforced: hence their self respect is positively altered. It would be heady wine indeed for a pupil who had never succeeded and was not liked by his mates or himself if he were given the opportunity to earn points for his chums.

Since this contingency would increase the interactions of the focal pupil and his peers, certain disadvantages could, of course, accrue. For example, a pupil who had a weak self concept might be given the opportunity to provide for his peers. If he did not perform, his peers might punish him and, consequently, he would be worse off than before.

GROUP CONSEQUENCE, CONTINGENT ON GROUP

When this approach is used the teacher must identify the same behavior for all group members, then count the frequency of those behaviors. Next, a consequence must be granted for the group if the frequency of the behavior was better than a specified level.

This group oriented system has been exemplified by the "good behavior game." Although a fair amount of research has been conducted using this technique, the original behavior game article was written by Barrish, Saunders, and Wolf (1969). Their study took place in a fourth grade classroom of 24 students. There were several youngsters in the class who had been sent to the principal for such problems as making disturbing noises, talking out of turn, or being out of seat.

Throughout the study two disruptive behaviors were targeted for daily measurement: out of seat occurrences and talk outs. Those behaviors were recorded for all members during a 30 minute reading and a 30 minute arithmetic period. In order to obtain data, observers used recording sheets divided into squares, each representing 1 minute. If any child engaged in either behavior, a check was made in the square assigned to that behavior. Observations were made once a minute.

During a baseline period when no special rule or contingency was associated with either talk outs or out of seats, it was reported that during reading and arithmetic, talk outs were indicated about 96% of the time and out of seat occurrences, 82% of the time.

Following a baseline period the game was introduced. First the class was divided by rows into two teams. The teacher then

———————◆———————

When this approach is used the teacher must identify the same behavior for all group members, then count the frequency of those behaviors. Next, a consequence must be granted for the group if the frequency of the behavior was better than a specified level. . . . This procedure has been referred to . . . as an *interdependent group contingency*.

———————◆———————

explained that out of seat incidents and talk outs were being recorded. The definitions of these behaviors were explained to the youngsters. The teacher also informed them that whenever one of them engaged in either behavior a mark would be placed on the chalkboard against his or her team. She informed them, too, that the team with the fewest marks at the end of the day would win. (Both teams could win if they had fewer than six marks.)

The members of the winning team would be allowed to wear victory tags, put stars by their names on the winners' chart (this chart was divided into two sections, one for each team), line up first for lunch if one team won (early, if both teams won), and take part at the end of the day in a 30 minute free period during which they could work on special projects. The youngsters were informed that the losing team would receive none of these privileges.

During the second condition of this experiment the game was in effect only during the math period. At that time the percentages of both target behaviors dropped considerably: 19% for talk outs and

9% for out of seats. Meanwhile, the percentages of those behaviors occurring in the reading period remained at the same levels as they were in the first part of the study.

Throughout the next condition, the game was not scheduled during math but was shifted to the reading sessions. At that time the percentages of the two behaviors during math rose to baseline proportions, but they decelerated significantly during reading.

In the final phase the game was reinstated for math and was kept in operation during reading. These data showed that the percentages for both behaviors were extremely low.

Another example of this technique was a study conducted by Sulzbacher and Houser (1968). Their investigation took place in a classroom of 14 mentally retarded youngsters, their ages ranging from 6½ to 10½.

The behavior of concern in the project was the "naughty finger": a raised fist with the middle finger extended. Throughout the study the teacher counted the frequency of this behavior and verbal references to it. During a 9 day baseline no unique effort was made to diminish the frequency of the target behaviors. On the average, 16 occurrences were noted.

Prior to the second phase, a set of 10 cards was mounted in the front of the room and numbered 10 through 1. It was explained to the children that there was to be a special 10 minute recess at the end of the day. Each time the teacher saw a "naughty finger," or heard reference to it, however, she turned a card over. At the end of the day they were given as many minutes for recess as were indicated by the card. Throughout this period, which lasted for 18 days, the frequency of the target behaviors was greatly reduced. Generally, there were only three incidents each day.

During an 8 day phase that followed, the cards and extra recess were removed. Correspondingly, the frequency of the behaviors increased.

This procedure has been referred to by Litow and Pumroy as an *interdependent group contingency*. Other experimenters, like Sulzbacher and Houser, achieved effective control of classroom behavior when the entire class was considered as one group (Grandy, Madsen, & De Mersseman, 1973; Schmidt & Ulrich, 1969; Simmons & Wasik, 1973; Wilson & Williams, 1973).

Other investigators, like Barrish et al., demonstrated that classroom behaviors were controlled when the class was divided into smaller groups (Harris & Sherman, 1973; Medland & Stachnik, 1972).

This contingency could be used to decelerate a wide variety of behaviors and might be arranged in situations other than regular classrooms. An acquaintance of mine employed this system with a group of 80 youngsters in a music class. She specified several inappropriate behaviors, divided the class in half, and counted each infraction. She entered the tallies for each group in her notebook and at the end of a week the group with the fewest points earned a party.

The music teacher's use of that contingency exemplifies the primary advantage of arranging contingencies for groups of children within a total class. She divided and conquered. In instances where several individuals are behaving inappropriately, it may be expedient to use this approach. Another benefit that might occur from its use with small groups would be that group loyalties might develop. When competitive situations are arranged across groups, pupils within those groups might become more supportive of one another.

The latter point might also prove to be a disadvantage in some situations, when either an entire class or groups within a class were involved. In many situations it is possible that either the group of youngsters is unable to win a prize or is punished unduly because of the behavior of a single individual. In those instances, the members who behave appropriately might retaliate by punishing the culprit or simply give up and cease relating to the group. In either event, the point of the group contingency would be defeated. When this has happened, some investigators have arranged individual contingencies for the few who could not participate as group members and group contingencies with the others. Barrish et al. arranged dual contingencies in their investigation because some youngsters could not function as group members.

4 Using the Techniques —A Final Word

The purpose of this monograph is to furnish teachers with several alternatives for managing the disruptive behaviors that may arise in their classes. In a final effort to insure that the management techniques described here will be used prudently and within the context of a developmental program, I am offering six further considerations.

DEFINING PRINCIPLES BY FUNCTION

This position has been stressed throughout the monograph, but it is important enough for one last explanation. Teachers must keep in mind that all the principles defined here (e.g., punishment, time out, extinction) attain that status only by function. If, for example, a teacher wanted to decelerate the frequency with which a boy hit others, he might scold him each time he pummeled his chums. If the frequency of that behavior remained unchanged, the teacher should label the technique as scolding. If, however, the frequency of the behavior diminished, the teacher should call it scolding *and* punishment. To extend the notion of functional definitions, the teacher should refer to the technique as positive reinforcement if the frequency of the hits increased after the scolding intervention.

One important reason for defining principles by function is that teachers are forced to explore more intently than they might otherwise do for the events that maintain behaviors. Let me explain. A teacher may have identified the talk outs of a boy as a particularly disruptive behavior, a behavior she intended to decelerate. Whereupon, she counted the frequency of the behavior during a baseline phase and concluded that the behavior, indeed, occurred too often. The teacher hypothesized that her attention to the behavior was the maintaining factor. She decided, therefore, to ignore the lad each time he talked out of turn. To her surprise, she learned the frequency of the talk outs was not lessened. Thus she had not used extinction, she merely used ignoring.

Determined to identify the reinforcer that maintained the talk outs, the teacher now theorized that the boy sitting next to the culprit was maintaining the disruptive behavior. She, therefore, told him to ignore his friend each time the latter talked out of turn. When this approach was arranged the talk outs diminished.

By using this searching process the teacher at last ascertained what event maintained the behavior, then withdrew it, and the behavior was extinguished. Had the teacher not identified principles by function, she might have decided that when her attention was removed that extinction was not appropriate. She might, as a result, attempt to use punishment or time out to eliminate the talk outs. If teachers define principles such as extinction, punishment, and for that matter, positive reinforcement, by their function, they will never be disappointed, for they will never fail. Only tactics such as ignoring, scolding, and giving M & M's can be disappointing.

EVALUATING TECHNIQUES

The only way to determine whether a technique is functional is to keep data. If, for example, a teacher wants to reduce the frequency with which a girl whines he should first define a whine. Once that is done he should count the number of times throughout the day that whining occurred. The teacher should count the whines for 3 or 4 days before rearranging the environment. One reason for obtaining these baseline data is to confirm whether or not the frequency is high enough to warrant further attention. Another reason for the baseline period is to focus the teacher's attention on the behavior so that he might learn which of several possible events is supporting the behavior.

After the baseline, if the teacher decides the frequency of the behavior is high enough to cause concern, he should change something in an effort to modify the behavior. He might either give something or take something away in his attempt to decelerate the behavior. He might arrange either an individual or a group oriented contingency. Whichever approach is chosen, the teacher should continue counting the frequency with which the behavior occurs.

By comparing the frequencies of the behavior during the baseline period to those during the treatment, the teacher would know whether or not the technique was effective, whether or not principle status had been attained.

CONSIDERING A VARIETY OF TECHNIQUES

Throughout this monograph several approaches have been considered, e.g., punishment or time out. In addition, it has been stressed that these approaches should be defined by their function, and the only way to do this is to keep data relevant to their effects.

With those considerations in mind it should be apparent that an infinite number of tactics comprise each principle. Take punishment, for example. If a teacher frowned at a boy each time he talked out of turn and the frequency of that behavior decelerated, frowning was punishing. Similarly, if she scolded, reminded, prompted, blinked, and behaviors associated with those events were extinguished, those actions were also punishing.

Too many teachers have associated electric shock with punishment. Although some studies have demonstrated that shock decelerated behaviors and was therefore a punisher, many other less potent events have diminished behaviors.

Just as many teachers associate punishment with electric shock, others connect time out with small, dark closets. Many have heard horror stories of children being placed in such enclosed spaces because of their disruptive behaviors, and have heard such rooms were called time out chambers. Many have considered the placement of children in such spaces as inhumane; they concluded, therefore, that time out was cruel, and subsequently vowed never to use it.

The point is that teachers can arrange time out situations without placing youngsters in small, dark rooms. When the definition of time

None of the principles can fail—only the tactics.

out is considered—the removal of the subject from a reinforcing environment—it can be seen that many events might serve the purpose. If, for example, pupils were removed from a music room, library, gymnasium, or lunch room contingent on behaviors and their frequencies lessened, those events were effective examples of time out.

Similarly, there are hundreds of tactics which might be used as response cost, differential reinforcement of a low rate of responding (DRL), differential reinforcement of other behaviors (DRO), overcorrection, or satiation approaches. To repeat, none of the principles can fail—only the tactics. Correspondingly, none of the principles are inherently good or evil; these evaluations are appropriate only for specific tactics.

COMBINING SOME TECHNIQUES

Many of the techniques mentioned here can well be combined. The advantage of blending approaches is that behaviors may thereby be modified quickly. The obvious disadvantage of merging techniques is that if effects are forthcoming, the manager does not know which approach was most influential, or whether, in fact, the total package was required. In spite of the scientific drawback of combining techniques, some groupings are often advised in clinical situations when behaviors must be modified quickly.

Several of the individually oriented approaches can be combined. Response cost and DRO might be used in an effort to reduce the frequency of talk outs. The teacher might give the child something for each 5 minute interval in which she did not talk out (DRO). Meanwhile, he could take away points each time she talked out (response cost).

Just as many of the individually oriented approaches may profitably be merged, likewise two group oriented systems might be arranged simultaneously. For instance, an interdependent contingency can be used with a dependent group contingency. A teacher might count each talk out for the group and if that number surpassed a certain level, all the youngsters would be denied recess (interdependent group contingency). Meanwhile, the teacher might give the entire class a minute of recess time each time a girl raised her hand before she asked a question (dependent group contingency).

Certainly group oriented and individually oriented systems can be in operation at the same time. I have mentioned earlier that often when interdependent group contingencies are established it is necessary to arrange individual contingencies for youngsters who cannot function as constituents of a group.

Teachers may also combine a decelerating approach with a technique designed to increase behaviors. One of the most common arrangements is to ignore disruptive behaviors and to reward appropriate behaviors. A teacher might praise a child when she is seated, and not attend to her when she is out of her chair. Correspondingly, a teacher might praise a child when she worked on her assignment and ignore her when she loafed.

USING SOME TECHNIQUES WITH ACADEMICS

Many of the techniques presented here to decelerate disruptive behaviors have been used to facilitate academic performances. For instance, punishment has been arranged on numerous occasions to decelerate errors. If a child misspelled or mispronounced a word, or incorrectly answered an arithmetic problem, she might be required to say or write the correct fact several times. If the frequencies of the errors diminished, those techniques would qualify as punishment because something was given (practice) in an effort to decelerate a behavior (committing errors).

Extinction might be arranged to eliminate certain behaviors in academic situations. Suppose, for example, a pupil, during a creative writing period, wrote more on bizarre themes than on realistic happenings. If the teacher wished to promote more of the latter and less of the former, he might comment lavishly on each sentence or phrase that was reasonable, and ignore totally all references to outlandish events.

We used response cost some years ago in an arithmetic study. In that project we took away 1 minute of recess time each time a girl incorrectly answered a subtraction problem. Prior to the withdrawal contingency she missed several problems each day. After the procedure was put in effect she rarely missed a problem.

Overcorrection has been used for years by music teachers. I can vividly recall that when I was assigned a song in the key of F and played B natural instead of B flat, my trumpet teacher required me not only to correct the wrong note but to play an entire phrase in which the note appeared.

Time out has also been used in academic situations. One instance comes to mind in which a boy was required to read each day from the Sullivan programed reading series. He was given one point for each five correct answers. The points were redeemable for minutes of free time. Since he enjoyed free time, the reading program was very reinforcing. Midway through one of the books he began to commit a few careless mistakes. The teacher promptly designed a plan to discourage that type of performance. In this new phase she shut his book for 1 minute each time he made an error. Thus, he was taken away from an environment that had been reinforcing. After a few days he ceased making careless errors.

The other individually oriented approaches might also be used in academic situations. Circumstances could be arranged whereby DRO, DRL, and satiation influenced performances in reading, handwriting, and mathematics.

Group oriented contingencies have been used to develop academic performances. A dependent group contingency was used by one researcher to increase a boy's spelling accuracy. In that study he was asked each day to spell a word. If he spelled it correctly, the entire class was given a few extra minutes during recess.

Independent group contingencies have been used by numerous researchers to accelerate academic performances. In those instances, each member was given something contingent on his or her performance in a selected academic area.

Interdependent group contingencies might also be scheduled to increase academic functioning. A situation could be arranged, for example, whereby all the group members were given extra recess time if all members of the group finished satisfactorily their arithmetic assignments.

Many of these individual or group oriented systems might well be combined with reinforcement procedures to further academic performance. In oral reading, for example, a child might be given a point for each 50 correctly read words. Furthermore, the child would be required to write each incorrectly pronounced word five times.

NEED TO DEVELOP BEHAVIORS

Although it may be necessary to decelerate certain behaviors, as has been mentioned before, this end must be accomplished within the context of a developmental program; for the primary mission of teachers is to teach. They must assist children to read, write, compute, to be independent, and to profit from their leisure time. The deceleration or elimination of behaviors such as out of seats and talk outs should be secondary to that assignment. Inappropriate behaviors should be dealt with only to the extent that they interfere with the current or future education of the individual who commits these behaviors or with the education and general well being of others in the immediate environment.

Sad to relate, some teachers hold the opinion that children would automatically be more productive if they engaged in fewer disruptive behaviors. Although some studies suggest such a relationship, others do not. Just as there is not always a direct relationship between disruptive behaviors and production, there is no definite correspondence between attending (appearing to be working) and production. Some research has reported that as attending increased so did production. Other investigations, however, have shown that the two behaviors were independent of one another.

There are children who are disruptive, who do not appear to attend to their work, but who finish their assignments satisfactorily. There are others who are never disruptive, who always seem to be working, yet never turn in their assignments.

The message to be gained from all of this is that teachers must not be deluded by phantom relationships. They should not suppose that school work will improve if attending is increased or disruptive behaviors are decreased. Generally, if teachers want to develop behaviors, they should focus their attention on these; if they intend to decelerate behaviors, they should concentrate on these. If, in the process, positive relationships do emerge, teachers should count their blessings, but they should not expect such generalized success the next time they program for a child.

References

Ayllon, T. Intensive treatment of psychotic behaviour by stimulus satiation and food reinforcement. *Behaviour Research and Therapy*, 1963, 1, 53–61.

Ayllon, T., & Roberts, M. D. Eliminating discipline problems by strengthening academic performance. *Journal of Applied Behavior Analysis*, 1974, 7, 71–76.

Azrin, N. H., & Powers, M. A. Eliminating classroom disturbances of emotionally disturbed children by positive practice. *Behavior Therapy*, 1975, 6, 525–534.

Baer, D. M., Wolf, M. M., & Risley, T. R. Some current dimensions of applied behavior analysis. *Journal of Applied Behavior Analysis*, 1968, 1, 91–97.

Barrish, H. H., Saunders, M., & Wolf, M. M. Good behavior game: Effects of individual contingencies for group consequences on disruptive behavior in a classroom. *Journal of Applied Behavior Analysis*, 1969, 2, 119–124.

Becker, W. C., Madsen, C. H., Jr., Arnold, C. R., & Thomas, D. R. The contingent use of teacher attention and praise in reducing classroom behavior problems. *Journal of Special Education*, 1967, 1, 287–307.

Birnbrauer, J. S., Bijou, S. W., Wolf, M. M., & Kidder, J. D. Programmed instruction in the classroom. In L. P. Ullmann & L. Krasner (Eds.), *Case studies in behavior modification*. New York: Holt, Rinehart & Winston, 1965.

Briskin, A. S., & Gardner, W. I. Social reinforcement in reducing inappropriate behavior. *Young Children*, 1968, 24, 84–89.

Brooks, R. B., & Snow, D. L. Two case illustrations of the use of behavior-modification techniques in the school setting. *Behavior Therapy*, 1972, 3, 100–103.

Carlson, C. S., Arnold, C. R., Becker, W. C., & Madsen, C. H., Jr. The elimination of tantrum behaviour of a child in an elementary classroom. *Behaviour Research and Therapy*, 1968, 6, 117–120.

Clark, H. B., Rowbury, T., Baer, A. M., & Baer, D. M. Timeout as a punishing stimulus in continuous and intermittent schedules. *Journal of Applied Behavior Analysis*, 1973, 6, 443-455.

Corte, H. E., Wolf, M. M., & Locke, B. J. A comparison of procedures for eliminating self-injurious behavior of retarded adolescents. *Journal of Applied Behavior Analysis,* 1971, *4,* 201-213.

Dietz, S. M., & Repp, A. C. Decreasing classroom misbehavior through the use of DRL schedules of reinforcement. *Journal of Applied Behavior Analysis,* 1973, *6,* 457–463.

Epstein, L. H., Doke, L. A., Sajwaj, T. E., Sorrell, S., & Rimmer, B. Generality and side effects of overcorrection. *Journal of Applied Behavior Analysis,* 1974, *7,* 385–390.

Foxx, R. M., & Azrin, N. H. The elimination of autistic self-stimulatory behavior by overcorrection. *Journal of Applied Behavior Analysis,* 1973, *6,* 1–14.

Grandy, G. S., Madsen, C. H., Jr., & De Mersseman, L. M. The effects of individual and interdependent contingencies on inappropriate classroom behavior. *Psychology in the Schools,* 1973, *10,* 488–493.

Greenberg, D. J., & O'Donnell, W. J. A note on the effects of group and individual contingencies upon deviant classroom behavior. *Journal of Child Psychology and Psychiatry,* 1972, *13,* 55–58.

Hall, R. V., Axelrod, S., Foundopoulos, M., Shellman, J., Campbell, R. A., & Cranston, S. S. The effective use of punishment to modify behavior in the classroom. *Educational Technology,* 1971, *11,* 24–26.

Hall, R. V., Fox, R., Willard, D., Goldsmith, L., Emerson, M., Owen, M., Davis, F., & Porcia, E. The teacher as observer and experimenter in the modification of disrupting and talking-out behaviors. *Journal of Applied Behavior Analysis,* 1971, *4,* 141-149.

Hall, R. V., Lund, D., & Jackson, D. Effects of teacher attention on study behavior. *Journal of Applied Behavior Analysis,* 1968, *1,* 1–12.

Harris, V. W., & Sherman, J. A. Use and analysis of the "Good Behavior Game" to reduce disruptive classroom behavior. *Journal of Applied Behavior Analysis,* 1973, *6,* 405–417.

Hart, B. M., Allen, K. E., Buell, J. S., Harris, F. R., & Wolf, M. M. Effects of social reinforcement on operant crying. *Journal of Experimental Child Psychology,* 1964, *1,* 145–153.

Iwata, B. A., & Bailey, J. S. Reward versus cost token systems: An analysis of the effects on students and teacher. *Journal of Applied Behavior Analysis,* 1974, *7,* 567–576.

Kaufman, K. F., & O'Leary, K. D. Reward, cost, and self-evaluation procedures for disruptive adolescents in a psychiatric hospital school. *Journal of Applied Behavior Analysis,* 1972, *5,* 293–309.

Kubany, E. S., Weiss, L. E., & Sloggett, B. B. The good behaviour clock: A reinforcement/time out procedure for reducing disruptive classroom behaviour. *Journal of Behaviour Therapy and Experimental Psychiatry,* 1971, *2,* 173–179.

Litow, L., & Pumroy, D. K. A brief review of classroom group-oriented contingencies. *Journal of Applied Behavior Analysis,* 1975, *8,* 341–347.

Lovitt, T. C. *In spite of my resistance, I've learned from children.* Columbus OH: Merrill, 1977.

Lovitt, T. C. Self-management projects with children with behavioral disorders. *Journal of Learning Disabilities,* 1973, *6,* 138–150.

Lovitt, T. C., Lovitt, A. O., Eaton, M. D., & Kirkwood, M. The deceleration of inappropriate comments by a natural consequence. *Journal of School Psychology,* 1973, *11,* 148–154.

Medland, M. B., & Stachnik, T. J. Good-behavior game: A replication and systematic analysis. *Journal of Applied Behavior Analysis*, 1972, 5, 45–51.

McAllister, L. W., Stachowiak, J. G., Baer, D. M., & Conderman, L. The application of operant conditioning techniques in a secondary school classroom. *Journal of Applied Behavior Analysis*, 1969, 2, 277–285.

Osborne, J. G. Free-time as a reinforcer in the management of classroom behavior. *Journal of Applied Behavior Analysis*, 1969, 2, 113–118.

O'Leary, K. D., Kaufman, K. F., Kass, R. E., & Drabman, R. S. The effects of loud and soft reprimands on the behavior of disruptive students. *Exceptional Children*, 1970, 37, 145–155.

Peterson, R. F., & Peterson, T. R. The use of positive reinforcement in the control of self-destructive behavior in a retarded boy. *Journal of Experimental Child Psychology*, 1968, 6, 351–360.

Phillips, E. L. Achievement Place: Token reinforcement procedures in a home-style rehabilitation setting for "pre-delinquent" boys. *Journal of Applied Behavior Analysis*, 1968, 1, 213–223.

Repp, A. C., & Deitz, S. M. Reducing aggressive and self-injurious behavior of institutionalized retarded children through reinforcement of other behaviors. *Journal of Applied Behavior Analysis*, 1974, 7, 313–325.

Risley, T. R. The effects and side effects of punishing the autistic behaviors of a deviant child. *Journal of Applied Behavior Analysis*, 1968, 1, 21–34.

Schmidt, G. W., & Ulrich, R. E. Effects of group contingent events upon classroom noise. *Journal of Applied Behavior Analysis*, 1969, 2, 171–179.

Schutte, R. C., & Hopkins, B. L. The effects of teacher attention on following instructions in a kindergarten class. *Journal of Applied Behavior Analysis*, 1970, 3, 117–122.

Simmons, J. T., & Wasik, B. H. Use of small group contingencies and special activity times to manage behavior in a first-grade classroom. *Journal of School Psychology*, 1973, 11, 228–237.

Sloane, H. N., Johnston, M. K., & Bijou, S. W. Successive modification of aggressive behavior and aggressive fantasy play by management of contingencies. *Journal of Child Psychology and Psychiatry*, 1967, 8, 217–226.

Sulzbacher, S. I., & Houser, J. E. A tactic to eliminate disruptive behaviors in the classroom: Group contingent consequences. *American Journal of Mental Deficiency*, 1968, 73, 88–90.

Watson, L. S. *How to use behavior modification with mentally retarded and autistic children*. Columbus OH: Behavior Modification Technology, 1972.

White, G. D., Nielsen, G., & Johnson, S. M. Time out duration and the suppression of deviant behavior in children. *Journal of Applied Behavior Analysis*, 1972, 5, 111–120.

Williams, C. D. The elimination of tantrum behavior by extinction procedures. *Journal of Abnormal and Social Psychology*, 1959, 59, 269.

Wilson, S. H., & Williams, R. L. The effects of group contingencies on first graders' academic and social behaviors. *Journal of School Psychology*, 1973, 11, 110–117.

Wolf, M. M., Hanley, E. L., King, L. A., Lachowicz, J., & Giles, D. K. The timer-game: A variable interval contingency for the management of out-of-seat behavior. *Exceptional Children*, 1970, 37, 113–117.

Wolf, M. M., Risley, T. R., & Mees, H. L. Application of operant conditioning procedures to the behaviour problems of an autistic child. *Behaviour Research and Therapy*, 1964, 1, 305–312.

Zimmerman, E. H., & Zimmerman, J. The alteration of behavior in a special classroom situation. *Journal of the Experimental Analysis of Behavior,* 1962, 5, 59–60.

 5710 268

A product of the ERIC Clearinghouse on Handicapped and Gifted Children.

 Published in 1978 by The Council for Exceptional Children, 1920 Association Drive, Reston, Virginia 22091

Library of Congress Number 78-54144

The material in this publication was prepared pursuant to a contract with the National Institute of Education, US Department of Health, Education, and Welfare. Contractors undertaking such projects under government sponsorship are encouraged to express freely their judgment in professional and technical matters. Prior to publication the manuscript was submitted to The Council for Exceptional Children for critical review and determination of professional competence. This publication has met such standards. Points of view, however, do not necessarily represent the official view or opinions of either The Council for Exceptional Children or the National Institute of Education.

Printed in the United States of America.

MANAGING INAPPROPRIATE BEHAVIORS IN THE CLASSROOM

Thomas C. Lovitt

What Research and Experience Say to the Teacher of Exceptional Children

THE COUNCIL FOR EXCEPTIONAL CHILDREN
MERNER-PFEIFFER LIBRARY
TENNESSEE WESLEYAN COLLEGE
ATHENS, TN 37303